THE
*Archive Photographs*
SERIES

# DENTON
AND
# HAUGHTON

Advert for the hatting firm Walker, Ashworth & Linney. At one time every man in Denton would wear a hat - turn up to work hatless and be sent home! Hatting was the main industry for the two towns and commanded great respect from its workers.

# THE Archive Photographs SERIES

# DENTON AND HAUGHTON

Compiled by
Jill Cronin
for
Denton Local History Society

CHALFORD

First published 1997
Copyright © Jill Cronin and the Denton Local History Society, 1997

The Chalford Publishing Company
St Mary's Mill, Chalford,
Stroud, Gloucestershire, GL6 8NX

ISBN 0 7524 0757 0

Typesetting and origination by
The Chalford Publishing Company
Printed in Great Britain by
Redwood Books, Trowbridge

*Dedication*
*In memory of our friend and local historian, Vera Howarth*

Dorothy and John Thompson getting into one of Redfern's taxis, 10 September 1951. Bill Redfern is the honeymooners' driver. The photograph is taken outside 104 Hyde Road, Denton. The houses opposite are now demolished and Oldham's canteen was built on the site.

# Contents

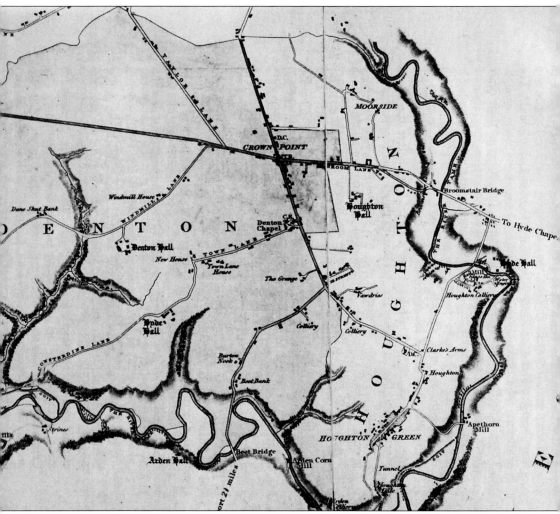

Johnson's Map, Denton and Haughton, 1820, showing the boundary between Denton and Haughton. The two towns merged in 1894 as Denton Urban District Council. Haughton Green still retains the name of the town, which once rivalled Denton in size and in population. There are various Haughtons in England. Note the misspelling of Haughton on this map. Denton Chapel was to become St Lawrence's Church.

# Introduction

Denton and its neighbour, Haughton, were originally small townships where the main occupation was farming. Situated about six miles east of Manchester in South Lancashire, within the vast parish and diocese of Manchester, they grew up side by side, rivalling each other in size and population until, in 1894, Haughton ceased to be a township and became part of Denton Urban District Council. Much of the land was owned by a few families, of whom the most important were the De Dentons and later the Hollands, who lived at Denton Hall, and the Hydes, who occupied the smaller residence of Hyde Hall. Denton Hall has been demolished but Hyde Hall still stands.

The name Denton means 'a village in a valley' and Haughton means 'a village on pieces of low-lying land by a river'. Both towns lie on the banks of the River Tame. Haughton covered the areas of Haughton, Haughton Green, Haughton Dale and Lower Haughton but today only Haughton Green retains this name.

Originally open moor which was gradually enclosed by the local landowners, the towns consisted of workers' cottages, mostly along the main roads or scattered over the fields and valleys. Woods abounded, such as Hulme's, Gibraltar, Horse Close and Hardy. Until the sixteenth century Denton and Haughton had no church, the people having to walk to neighbouring Stockport or Manchester to worship, but around 1530 the leading landowners built a chapel of ease known as St James' Chapel. After renovation in the nineteenth century it was renamed St Lawrence's Church.

During the civil war (1642-49) between Charles I and Parliament, Colonel Richard Holland of Denton Hall and Robert Hyde of Hyde Hall took part in the successful defence of Manchester against the king's supporters. As well as firearms and pikes, many of their followers carried scythes and pitchforks, the weapons of a farming community. By this time however, industry on a small scale had reached the area when Flemish Huguenots brought their glassmaking skills to Haughton. Their early coal fired furnace for glassmaking was built in Glass House Fold, where fine glass was produced for many years. This fold was excavated and recorded by archaeologists in the early 1970s. The glassmakers' names live on in the parish registers of Stockport and Ashton-under-Lyne and in their descendants in the town; the name De Howe was especially popular.

Coal for the furnace came from the rich local coal seams and the earliest written reference to coal-mining dates to 1571. By 1851, 175 boys and men from Haughton alone worked in the mines; at one time there were about twenty-three named coal pits in the two towns. Denton Colliery (earlier called Burton Nook) and Great Wood were the last pits. Denton Colliery closed in 1929, after being damaged by flooding during strikes. A tramway had opened in 1853, linking first Burton Nook and then Great Wood Pits with the coal wharf at Reddish and the London and North Western Railway Company line. There was also a pumping station for the mines at Hulme's Wood and a mines rescue station on Stockport Road.

There were never many cotton mills in the two towns, although in 1851 almost half of Haughton's workforce was employed in cotton; often whole families worked in the mills. Denton had only one mill, Alpha, and Haughton but a few. The workers travelled from Denton to the surrounding towns and today no mills remain in Denton.

Hatting, the industry for which Denton was to become famous, started as a sideline for certain enterprising farmers who used the fur from the abundant rabbit population to make hats. Eventually, small hatting businesses were set up by the middle of the nineteenth century. All the large firms exported to Europe. In 1851, 244 men and 99 women worked in hatting just in Haughton. The Census shows a varied set of workers, ranging from hatmasters to skilled blockers, dyers, finishers and trimmers. Slow to use machinery and quick to strike, the workers saw a slump in the 1850s but silk hatting helped to produce a market again. By 1904 the prosperity of the end of the century, produced by the fashionable Homburg and Trilby hats, was on the wane. Mechanisation was almost complete, although trimming was still a skilled handicraft. Changes in fashion after the war were the death knell for hatting in the area and the Denton Hat Company was the last to close in recent years.

Hatting brought prosperity to Denton. Houses for the workers were built and whole communities grew up near to the large hatting works. The preparation of the fur and the production of the machinery for hatting developed as separate industries. This prosperity was reflected in the building of large churches, such as Christ Church, and its schools in the mid-nineteenth century. Another fine church was built in Haughton in 1882 by the Sidebothams, a local family of cotton manufacturers and mineowners. St Anne's Church and Rectory were designed by the unusual architect, Medland Taylor. In 1874 he had also designed St Mary's Church in Haughton Green. This church was endowed by the local wire works owner, James Walton, in memory of his daughter, Mary, as St Anne's was named after Joseph Sidebotham's wife and also his mother.

Although the old industries have disappeared, Denton still has a world famous firm: Oldham's. Founded in 1865 to make machinery for the hatting trade and later miners' lamps, it now specialises, as Oldham Crompton, in the production of batteries. Another early industry, brick making, still continues in Windmill Lane, although the former Jackson's Brick Works no longer uses clay extracted in Denton.

Communications have grown up mainly by road. Denton centre at Crown Point is bisected by two main roads: Hyde to Manchester and Ashton to Stockport. Once toll gates forced travellers to pay for the use of most of these thoroughfares. Until recently Haughton Green still had its green, with houses clustered around it and Denton's town centre was originally in Town Lane in an area known as 'The City' near Denton Hall and St Lawrence's Church. Canals never reached Denton, although an unfinished one was begun in the Tame Valley. The railway passes through the town but its station is barely used now. In recent years the motorway has bisected the town as part of the motorway link around Manchester.

Today the prosperity produced by hatting, mining and cotton is still evident in the local amenities and public buildings. The parks, libraries, Town Hall and Festival Hall are proof of this, as are the churches, schools, clubs and public houses. In 1645 the combined population of Denton and Haughton was 290, in 1891 it had grown to 14,000 and it now stands at some 38,000. Since 1974 Denton has been in Tameside Metropolitan Borough but, in many ways, it still retains much of its old character and community spirit.

The photographs in this book are just a selection of the hundreds collected and saved over the past nineteen years by the Denton Local History Society and stored in their archive. Some of the photographs, taken by the eminent early photographer Joseph Sidebotham, come from the important collection owned by St Anne's Church, Haughton. The selection includes many societies, sports teams, clubs and special events such as the Whit Walks. As well as the buildings of Denton and Haughton, the photographs portray the people of the area at work, at leisure and at home, in times of war and of peace.

# One

# From Town to Country

The Avenue, Ross Lave Lane, Denton, early 1900s. This is a well-known lane, lined with trees, which links Town Lane with Hyde Hall, Denton. The hall, once a farm and then a stables, was originally the family home of the Hyde family, who also had halls in Hyde and North America.

Crown Point, Denton, *c.* 1915, looking from Manchester Road east to Hyde Road. Tram lines and a tram are visible and the King's Head Pub is on the right, opposite the Red Lion, which is on the corner of Stockport and Hyde Roads. The Red Lion was once the stopping off point for the long distance mail coaches. It was also the centre for journeymen hatters looking for work.

Crown Point, Denton, in the late 1950s, looking west along Manchester Road; Christ Church is visible on the horizon. Trolley bus lines have replaced the tram tracks. The King's Head Pub is on the left and the Exchange was on the right on Ashton Road. Crown Point was named after the British victory in North America in 1759.

Stockport Road, Denton, going south, away from Crown Point, 1957. Hope Congregational Church is on the right. It began life in a cottage by the Market Ground, was built in 1836 on Stockport Road and when that became the school in 1877, this church was built. Denton Police Station is the tall building further along on the right. Originally there was an old court house with its cellar jail on Town Lane, in an area called 'The City'.

Ashton Road, looking north from Crown Point. Notice the policeman on duty in the middle of the crossroads. The Exchange Inn was near the east corner of Ashton Road and the shop next to it was Catlow's newsagents. There were two milestones to Hyde and to Ashton.

Broomstair, Hyde Road, Haughton, c. 1908, looking east toward Hyde and Broomstair Bridge across the River Tame. The Lowe's Arms is on the left. Until 1818 the original main road, Old Broom Lane, ran behind the Lowe's Arms and down to a ford across the river. The coat of arms of the Lowe family was used as the sign.

Hyde Road, Haughton, looking west to Crown Point, 1930s. The Angel Hotel, licensed in about 1597, was refurbished in the 1970s. On its wall is a milestone, indicating 6 miles to Manchester and 1 mile to Hyde. Opposite the pub is a row of shops called Jamaica Terrace; the tramway ran along Hyde Road. The Angel was once a coaching inn and the bricked up entrance to the stables can be seen to the right of the front door. Originally this would have been the back as the old main road, Old Broom Lane, ran behind here.

Lane from Arden Hall, leading down to Stockport Road, Denton, around 1916. The house in the centre behind the children was once a pub called the Horseshoe Inn and lies by the bridge crossing the Tame and joining Denton with Bredbury.

Cottages in Hulme's Wood, Denton, *c.* 1908. These miners' cottages are now demolished. The wood lies behind Denton Cemetery, on the banks of the Tame. A pumping station for Hulme's Pit was sited in the wood.

Reddish Vale, Denton, by the River Tame, around 1910. This river meanders around Denton and Haughton and forms the boundary between Denton and Reddish to the west, Bredbury to the south and Audenshaw to the north. It was the old border between Cheshire and Lancashire.

Reddish Vale lies between Denton and Reddish on a flood plain. The scene is virtually unchanged today and is a pleasant place to walk.

Three old wells on Dark Lane, Haughton. These were an early source of fresh water for the inhabitants of Glass House Fold. The lane is now better known as Mill Lane and joins Hyde with Haughton Green. The wells were to the left, 100 yards nearer Haughton Green than the Fold, and were used until Dark Lane was widened in 1922. They are also known as Catherine Wells.

The reservoirs, 1910, viewed from Debdale Park, which lies on the borders of Denton and Gorton. These reservoirs once supplied Gorton, Denton and Audenshaw but some of them have also been used for leisure activities.

A favourite walk between the reservoirs, 1902, which served Gorton, Denton and Audenshaw. This photograph is taken from the Gorton end looking towards Hyde.

A later view of this walk, 1916.

A horse and cart in the early 1900s, transporting a group dressed up for an outing. The scene is Manchester Road, Denton, but the houses have since been demolished, including the shop selling Taylor's Eagle Ales. Nearby was Manchester Road Methodist Church and Seymour Street.

A horse and cart at work before 1914. John Thompson & Son ran a saw mill in Patterson Street, off Hyde Road, Denton. The cases on the cart were probably for delivery to a local hat works or for delivery to Denton Station after being made up at a hat works; these would be for ladies' hats. Thompson's built Walker, Ashworth & Linney's Hat Works. (see page 28)

Horse following a cart, Ashton Road, Denton. Notice the contrast of the tram further along the road. The Exchange Inn is front right.

Charabanc outing from Broomstair Paper Mill, which is seen in the background and which operated by the River Tame on Watson Street, Haughton. Each gentleman sports a hat, as befits a hatting town. The style is that of the early 1920s. The charabanc is the 'boneshaker' type with metal wheels.

Charabanc outing from Oldham & Sons Ltd. The Oldham family produced miners' lamps and hatting machinery from 1865 and employed many local people. The 'Buy Victory Loan' posters on the left state 'To reduce the cost of living'. Together with the Union Jacks, this dates the photograph to around 1918. The excursion was probably to the seaside.

An Ashton bound tram outside the Angel Hotel, Haughton, *c.* 1914, which was owned by Openshaw Brewery at this time. The Angel has been altered many times from its original sixteenth century building. In the distance can be seen the chimney of Nathan Wild's Hat Works.

The tram office on Manchester Road, Denton, c. 1960. A clock stood in the window and the tram conductors clocked in and brewed up there. About 1,920 parcels came there by tram and were then delivered by a parcel boy with a wicker trolley.

A No. 57 tram bound for Ashton, 1940s. The scene is the corner of David Street and Two Trees Lane, opposite the Cock Hotel.

A No. 217 Manchester Corporation trolley bus at the terminus at Haughton Green in the 1960s. These buses used the same terminus that the trams had used.

Denton Station, crowded for a special outing. This would probably be for the Wakes Week holiday, when many Dentonians would travel by train to Blackpool. Sadly, Denton Station is now virtually unused.

The staff at Denton Station. They would be saddened to see the deserted and derelict station of today.

The staff at Denton Station, 1962. In the centre is Councillor Ronald Martin who was Chairman of Denton Urban District Council from May 1961 to May 1962. Here he is visiting the railway workers. From left to right: Eric ?, Albert Chadderton, Frederick Whiteside, William Sheeran.

A row of Oldham's vans outside Peacock Lodge, 1930s. This stood at the corner of Lime Grove and Annan Street. Once the home of the Peacocks, a hatting family, it became part of Oldham & Sons Ltd. The delivery vans sport the Oldham logo and address.

Another Oldham's delivery vehicle outside the houses in Annan Street, which belonged to the Howe family, who had their hat factory next door. The railings are long gone for the war effort. The end of this Manchester-made lorry can be seen in the photograph above.

*Two*

# Hatting

Dane Bank Farm and hat works, usually called Woolfendens after the family who ran the business. The farmhouse still stands although it ceased to be a farm in 1943. The last tenants were the Swindells and the Bennetts. The hat factory, with its workers' houses, shop and pub is sadly demolished. The owners and managers' houses still stand as High Bank Houses.

*The Howe letter-heading, with its proud boast "The oldest makers of felt hats in England."*

Advert for Howe's hats, Annan Street, Denton. In 1710 Howes began hatting in Annan, Scotland, but in 1838 Joseph Howe, a dyer, set up a large factory in Denton, naming the street after his native town. He began by delivering dyed hats on a donkey. His six sons entered the firm and enlarged the factory onto Amelia Street. The factory closed in 1973.

The chimney and hat factory of Joseph Howe & Sons Ltd, Annan Street, Denton, 1979. Hat factory chimneys are very distinctive with a circular brick tower and a square brick base. The building was designed to be converted easily to housing if business failed. The factory was demolished in 1996.

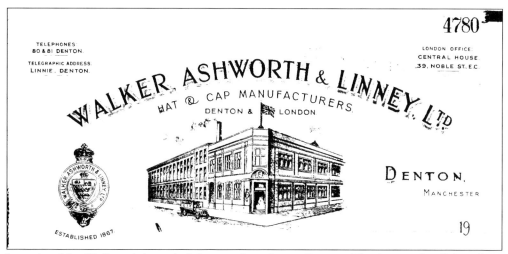

TELEPHONES
80 & 81 DENTON.

TELEGRAPHIC ADDRESS.
LINNIE. DENTON.

LONDON OFFICE
CENTRAL HOUSE.
39. NOBLE ST. E.C.

WALKER, ASHWORTH & LINNEY, LTD

HAT & CAP MANUFACTURERS.
DENTON & LONDON

DENTON.
MANCHESTER

ESTABLISHED 1867.

19

Letterhead for Walker, Ashworth & Linney, Law Street, Denton. The firm made silk hats from 1867, when silk hats made a comeback for hatting and competed with felt hats.

The coat of arms of Walker, Ashworth & Linney. These were proudly displayed on either side of the office doorway on the corner of Ashton Road and Law Street, Denton. They also stood on top of the building facing Ashton Road and were the firm's trade mark.

27

Offices of Walker, Ashworth & Linney on the corner of Ashton Road and Law Street, Denton. This photograph was taken in July 1978 prior to demolition for the M67 motorway. Notice the clock and coat of arms on the top of the building and the large coats of arms on either side of the doorway. The three storey workshop is to the left. The offices were built by Thompson's. (see page 17)

The workshops and offices of Walker, Ashworth & Linney, silk hat makers, in Law Street, Denton in July 1978. Notice the two storey works which could be turned into houses if the firm failed. The bricks under the windows were left ready to be made into the doors to the houses.

## It may not be quite like this . . .

### but 'Attaboy' hats are the fastest sellers

Hat sales certainly go up when you stock 'Attaboy.' Its sensible combination of price and quality gives the customer just what he wants today. That is why 'Attaboy' still leads the market by a large margin and continues to keep sales moving.

## HATTING'S BEST SELLER

*Issued by the Denton Hat Co. Ltd., Denton, Nr. Manchester.* M-W.84

An advert issued by the Denton Hat Company, Wilton Street, Denton, to advertise a popular style of hat, the Attaboy. This was created by Mr Harry Greenhough at the Vinery Hat Works on Town Lane. He moved to Wilton Street as the Denton Hat Company in 1932. This was the origin of the catchphrase, 'If you want to get ahead, get a hat'. This advert appeared in *Men's Wear*, 22 October 1955.

Wool forming at Lancashire Felt Co., Denton, before 1914. The company came into hatting late and eventually developed into Lancaster Carpets. Wool was used to blend with rabbit or beaver fur in layers to start the hatting process. The firm specialised in wool and fur hoods which were then completed as hats elsewhere.

Fur forming at the Lancashire Felt Co., Denton, before 1914. The wool and fur were pressed into a conical shape which was far larger than the hat would be. These were called hoods.

Steaming soft felts at Walker, Ashworth & Linney in March 1923. The conical hoods were reduced in size and given shape by a process called planking. This involved hot water and sulphuric acid plus a rolling pin; the hat was then shaped on a wooden block. The sons ran the company which became a limited company in 1912.

Hat making at Walker, Ashworth & Linney Ltd in March 1923.

This family photograph reveals a planking shop behind 87 Hyde Road, Haughton, c. 1949. Planking shops were always situated at the back of houses where the family could carry out the difficult and dangerous process of steaming the hat hoods into shape using hot water and various chemicals. This one has now been demolished. The lady is May White.

Workers in the planking department of Wilson's hat shop, *c.* 1908, situated on Wilton Street, Denton. The gentleman second from the right at the front is Robert Bromley, a long-standing member of Denton Original Prize Band. He played the French horn both before and after the First World War.

Carlton Hat Factory, Moorside Lane, Haughton, *c.* 1913. James Brown, a hat presser and shaper, works at his machine. This firm was later called Gledhill Robinson, after the owner.

Trimmers busy at work in a hat factory, Denton. Originally trimming was carried out at home by women but eventually they too became part of the factory scene.

Howe's Hat Works in 1971. Ladies' hats are on display. Hat firms showed their wares at various venues, one of which was at the Denton Show in the Festival Hall, Denton. Evident here are uniform hats, including nurses and St John Ambulance, and also dress hats.

Workers outside Bevan's Hat Factory on Stockport Road. The ladies would be trimmers who put the finishing touches to the hats. Originally they worked at home and the hats were carried to and from the factory.

The warehouse staff outside Moore's Hat Factory, pre-1914. Few photographs exist of these workers in hat factories. The lady in the front row on the left is Doris Thewlis. Moore's factory still stands on Heaton Street, off Manchester Road, Denton, and was a huge complex of buildings.

Byrom Meadowcroft, 1932. Here he is carrying a pile of men's hats across the yard of Moore's Hat Works. In his spare time he was a lay preacher at Two Trees Lane and Hyde Road Methodist Churches.

The demolition of Nathan Wild's Hat Works on Broomgrove Lane, Haughton. The chimney was the last part to be demolished on 19 June 1978. The hat works had become a garage known as Polygon Works and lay just behind St Anne's School. This part of the firm was known as the 'bottom or finishing end'. The other part was in Old Broom Lane and was called the 'wet end'.

# Three
# At Work: from Farming to Shopping

Yew Tree Farm, demolished 1899. This was a timber framed farmhouse off Stockport Road, Denton. Now the houses of Yew Tree housing estate stand where its farmhouse and fields once lay. The drawing is by Vera Howarth.

Newhouse Farm and hat works. This farm lay on Town Lane, Denton, where the road bends towards Hyde Hall. It was a strange building. A third storey was added to make it into a hat works and the deep advanced porch was built up in the form of a tower.

Newhouse Farm with Doris Healey on the right, c. 1930. The datestone reads 'TL EL 1667' and probably refers to Thomas Lees and his wife Elizabeth. The doors of the house were at one time perforated after the style of loopholes. This was said to have been done for musketry at a time of siege, when one branch of the Lees family held the house against another.

The milk cart of Alfred Leak, farmer at Haughton Hall Farm, Haughton, *c.* 1930s. Haughton Hall was probably the home of the Haughton family. It was a black and white half timber framed hall. On its lintel was 'TB MB 1678', referring to the Booth family. Part of it was rebuilt in brick in 1723. In the nineteenth century John Bentley, a hatter, owned it and the timber part was demolished in the 1870s. The boy is Albert Arrowsmith and the man Tommy Pollitt, who worked as a farmhand.

Thorpe Lane Farm, Haughton, in the 1930s. Farms were often named after their farmers and this one was called Broome's. Here Mr Broome is haymaking, helped by his daughter, son-in-law, grandchildren and two farm labourers. In the distance can be seen Moorside Farm, which was farmed by Mr Wagstaff at that time.

Lewis Bowden's farm, pre-1890. This farm stood on the corner of Bowden Street and Manchester Road, Denton. Now the Liberal Club stands on the site.

The other side of Bowden's Farm, pre-1890.

# ANNIE B. BROOME.

## LEES HOUSE FARM.

## TOWN LANE, DENTON.

### PURE NEW MILK DELIVERED DAILY, DIRECT

### FROM THE FARM,

### NEW LAID EGGS.

Lees House Farm, Town Lane, Denton. This is an advert from the 1930s. Most farms in the area kept animals. The land had not grown crops since early days, as the hard clay of the area is unsuitable for arable farming. On the lintel 'REL 1720 IL' is inscribed, referring to Robert and Elizabeth Lee, with their son, John.

Wedding photograph, Lees House Farm, 22 August 1918. Minnie Broome is seen here on her wedding day. In the front row, second on the left, is Annie Broome. This picture was taken at the rear of the farmhouse.

Gibraltar Mill, c. 1853. This photograph was taken by a gifted amateur photographer, Joseph Sidebotham, in the days of early photography. Another photographer is caught in the foreground, seen as a double image because of the time lapse with early cameras. He is possibly Joseph Mudd, a well known photographer and friend of Joseph's. Joseph's great grandfather had brought the family to this area in the eighteenth century. This William Sidebotham of Hyde had four sons and between them, they built five of the area's mills: Gibraltar, Haughton Dale (Meadow), Apethorn, Kingston and Moorfield (later Tayler Bros.). They also erected beautiful homes for their families: Kingston Hall and Apethorn, Haughton Dale (Victoria Place), Hoviley and Rose Bank Houses. The family also acquired Shepley Hall and two collieries – the Broomstair and the Hyde and Haughton.

Gibraltar Mill, Gibraltar Lane. This mill was built in 1760 across the River Tame in Gee Cross by John Sidebotham. It employed many Denton and Haughton cotton workers. In 1967 it was demolished. The view is taken looking down Gibraltar Lane and across Gibraltar Bridge to the mill. Nearby was Apethorn House, one of the Sidebotham homes.

Meadow or Haughton Dale Mill was built in 1790 as a cotton mill, by John Sidebotham, usually called John of Hoviley. Later, in 1853, it became a wire works and was owned by James Walton. He was an inventor in the field of wire-drawing and card-making. The mill closed in 1903 and was demolished. Only the remodelled lodge can now be seen.

Workers at a Haughton Dale cotton mill.

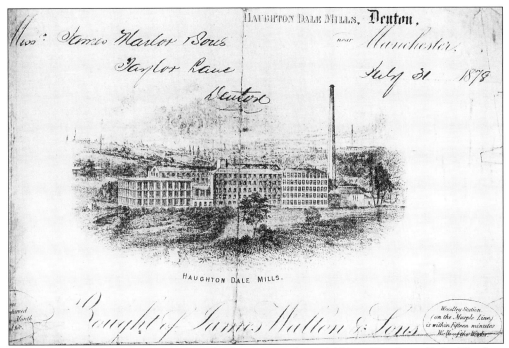

Letter heading used by James Walton for his wire works in 1878 at Haughton Dale. The line drawing makes the works look very impressive to the letter reader. The bill is also interesting because it was sent to Charles Marlor, a member of the Marlor family, who were hatters in Marlor Street, Denton.

Alpha Mill, Denton, 22 April 1915. This was Denton's only cotton mill, opened in 1862. Shown here is the second of at least three major fires there. It later became a chemical works and burned down in a disastrous fire in 1920. Three men were killed when an explosion blew off the roof and destroyed the walls.

45

The pithead of Broomstair Colliery, Hyde Road, Haughton, c. 1970. It was owned by the Bradbury family and later the Sidebotham family, together with the Hyde and Haughton Colliery.It closed at the end of the nineteenth century because of flooding. Two miners had already been almost drowned on being lowered down the shaft on 1 January 1899. This pit's demise led to the closure of mines in Dukinfield.

Hulme's Wood Pumping Station. This helped to pump out water from the pits. It was originally a coal pit but was adapted to a pumping station with a Newcomen engine when flooding was a problem. Capable of delivering water from a depth of 420 feet, it consumed 3 tons of coal a week. It fell into disuse after the closure of Denton Colliery in 1929-30 and has now been excavated.

Denton Colliery office staff in 1916.

The Bogie Lines, Denton. There was a special mineral tramway built in 1853 for Denton Colliery as a branch line to transport the coal to the depot at Reddish and so onto the London and North Western Railway Company line. This photograph is taken from Hyde Hall Bridge.

Denton Colliery, Stockport Road, Denton, *c.* 1954, prior to demolition. Three Lane Ends is on the left. The two buildings on the left are the two engine sheds for the colliery locos, *Nancy* and *Denton*. Next to them is the archway to the colliery winding gear and beside that sleepers fence off the mine shaft which was filled-in and closed in 1965. The mound is The Bank, the slag heap where horse drawn wagons loaded up onto the lorries. The nearer building was the colliery office (now a stonemason's) and the further building was the Mine Rescue Station (now two houses and a bungalow). The holes in the foreground are the result of pit waste digging during the 1926-27 strikes.

George Shaw & Partners Ltd in the 1940s. This firm made hatting sundries and imported hatters' furs, linings, galloons and the like. Situated in Market Street, Denton, opposite the Town Hall, it was established in 1880 and is now no longer operating.

Advert for John Turner, hatting machine inventor and maker, which appeared in the *Hatters' Gazette*, 1886. John Turner of Denton and Giles Atherton of Stockport joined forces to invent and produce machinery for hatting. Their works still stand on the corner of Ashton Road and Turner Street, Denton. Originally it was called the White House Company and the White House Public House still stands opposite it.

Works outing from Turner Atherton Ltd, *c.* 1930s. The workers are waiting outside the White House on Ashton Road, near to the firm. Leonard Nield is fourth from the left. The sign reads, 'Offilers Nut Brown Ales'.

50

Nelson Street, Denton. This road still exists but is no longer a public thoroughfare. It was fenced off by Oldham & Sons Ltd, whose buildings can be seen here. The road runs from Hyde Road near Crown Point towards Annan Street. In the distance can be seen the edge of Howe's Hat Works on the left and their family houses on the right.

Joseph and his son Orlando Oldham, with their first planking machine, c. 1886, which was worked by hand. The firm was established in 1882 on Hyde Road after moving from various other sites in Denton. Oldham & Sons invented hatting machinery and then became world famous for miners' lamps.

A typical scene in Oldham & Sons Ltd, 1914-18. The women had to cope with turning out the shell cases during the First World War.

Wireless accumulator production at Oldham & Sons Ltd, Denton, during the early 1930s.

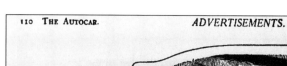

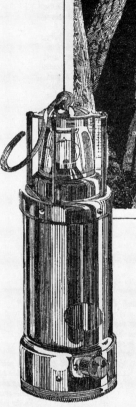

*Oldham Miner's Lamp.*

## Do you know a more stren-uous test for any Battery than this?

EVEN the motorist who has never descended a pit-shaft must readily realise the strenuous conditions down below  Faced with eight hours of hard toil, often at a considerable distance in the interior of the mine itself, it is small wonder that the miner attaches the greatest importance to his lamp

Years ago the only lamp available was the old Davy—a lamp burning paraffin. Now, thanks to the foresight and perseverance of such firms as Oldham and Son Ltd., the majority of pits have discarded the Davy lamp in preference to an electric lamp.  As a matter of fact, Oldham Miner's Lamps actually outnumber all the other electric lamps in the country added together.

But the evolution of the Oldham Lamp was not achieved over-night.  It took many years of patient endeavour to produce a Lamp—and especially an accumulator—that could withstand hard knocks and at the same time yield a steady output month in and month out.

Its ultimate success is due entirely to the method of plate manufacture—**the special activation process**—which is an exclusive Oldham feature.

This process is now being applied to Lighting and Starting Batteries with great success. Obviously the battery that can survive the rigorous conditions of service below ground will make child's play of cranking up a sulky engine on a winter's morning.

## OLDHAM
### Special  activation  process

The Advertisement Index is on the Second Page Preceding the Classified Advertisements.  37

An advert for Oldham's in *Autocar* 17 October 1924. In the early days of motoring such an unorthodox approach was effective. This advert shows the miners' lamp, which made Oldham's famous.

Sturtevant Engineering Company, Acre Street, Denton, 1946-7. Here a Fordson tractor is powering lineshafts during a power cut caused by the Second World War. Sturtevants specialised in the production of fans for factories, including the ventilation fans for the Mersey Tunnel.

Sturtevant Engineering Company, March 1945. In this general view of the machine shop, note all the lineshafts. The firm closed in 1984 and housing now covers the site. Bill Garrett is in the centre.

E. Pass and Company, Denton, specialists in underpressure engineering, c. 1960. The firm was in Holland Street but is now closed down. Here they exhibit their products, as they did at home and also abroad.

E. Pass and Company, 1954. Again they exhibit their wares, including valves and engineering accessories, at Malvern.

St Anne's Laundry at Henfold Farm, Denton, established in 1898. This farm in Town Lane was combined with the family-run laundry. Washing was collected on Monday and returned on Friday. The horses which pulled the cart were called Daisy and Billy.

Mrs Sally Miles working at the laundry at the open air drying.

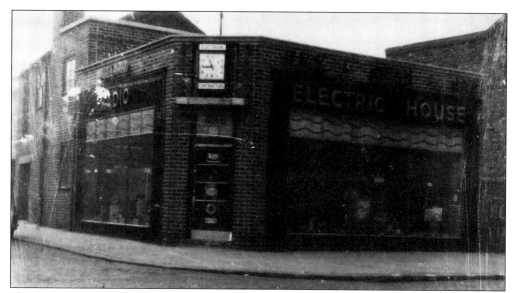

Electric House at the corner of Ashton Road and Annan Street. In about 1946 this shop and works were built for Percy Barr, an electrical contractor and retailer. In the early 1950s the Co-op bought the building. Mr Barr moved his shop to where the Britannia Building Society now stands and his works to the corner of Acre Street and Town Lane. Electric House was one of the largest electrical contractors in the country.

J. Blackwell, cycle shop, Denton. Later this became Northend's on Hyde Road and is now on Lime Grove.

Burgon's Ltd on Manchester Road, on the north side near Peel Street, were a high class grocers, established in 1847. They sold Doctor China's tea ('your doctor recommends it!'), Australian eggs and, of course, Oxo, among many other things. Notice the delivery boy's bicycle outside the shop for home deliveries. Mr Edwards is in the doorway.

Plant's shop at Crown Point, c. 1947, showing the Whit Walk procession. This photograph was used to sell the shop and had the following information on its back. It had been rebuilt 35 years before. Now it had been measured up by a Mr France. Length Manchester Road side 57 feet 6 inches, including yard. 3 windows on this side, including stock room. Width, Ashton Road side, 20 feet, narrowing to about 13 feet. 2 large windows on this side. 1 smaller window in stock room. 5 windows in all. It was built about 1912.

Crown Point Supper Bar on Hyde Road, Denton. *c.* 1900s, was to the right of Saxon Street. The poster in the window offers a £200 reward - a lot of money in those days.

The Co-operative Society, Haughton Green branch, 1923. The society had quite a few branches in the area, including a large central store on Hyde Road, Denton. All these shops are now closed. The Haughton branch was established in 1875.

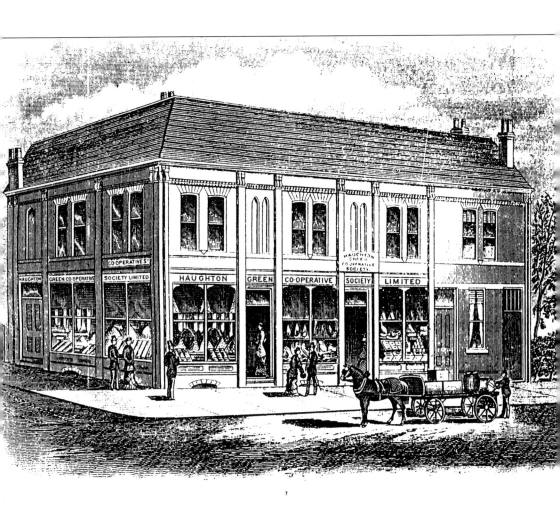

# Haughton Green Equitable Co-operative Society, Ltd

### ESTABLISHED 1875.

Haughton Green Co-operative Society, established 1875. This report of 8 December 1923 announces a half year's sales of £20,060 3s 5d. The lucky customers would receive a divi of 2/3d in the £ on grocery etc. and 1/3d on butchery.

# Four

# Housing from Halls to Cottages

Wood carving, east wing, Denton Hall, 23 September 1978. This is the only remaining corner decoration out of probably four ceiling carvings in the ground floor hall, possibly depicting the Green Man, an early fertility symbol, usually shown with vine leaves coming out of his mouth. This wing may originally have been the chapel and was built partly over the moat of an earlier hall.

View of Denton Hall, 1870. This is the main wing which housed a great hall. The west wing was demolished in 1894; the left hand side burned down in the 1930s and the east wing stood on the left side of the hall. The De Denton family first owned the original hall and by marriage passed it on to the Hollands and then to the Egertons, who became the Earls of Wilton.

Denton Hall, after 1894. This shows the main wing, minus the west wing, which was demolished in 1894.

Removal of the east wing, Denton Hall, Friday 1 June 1979. The west side of the roof is here being lowered onto a lorry to be transported to Alderley Edge and then re-erected as a private museum for vintage cars. The old hall had become a farm and the timber framed east wing had been encased in brick and used as barns.

The courtyard of Arden Hall, Castle Hill, 1743. Although just over the border in Bredbury, this hall is part of Denton's history and the Arden family played their part in the town's past. It was once moated and a battle is said to have taken place on Castle Hill beside the hall between the Cavaliers and Roundheads.

The entrance to Arden Hall. Here a young girl poses by the gate. The moat can still be seen near to this gateway.

ARDEN HALL

NEAR DENTON (NO. 1).

Arden Hall. A young boy stands in front of the hall's main tower.

Hyde Hall, off Town Lane, Denton, 1910. The Hyde family had halls in both Denton and Hyde. This hall still stands at the end of the Avenue. (see page 9) Recently a stables and once a farm, it possesses a great hall, seen here from its exterior on the garden side.

Hyde Hall, Denton. This was originally a black and white half timbered hall inhabited by the Hydes of Denton. They were a younger branch of the Hydes of Hyde, who owned land in Denton back in the thirteenth century. Notice the mounting block for the use of riders.

Denton Lodge, (Peacock Lodge), Denton, built in 1790 by the Peacock family, local hat manufacturers. This was one of the largest houses in Denton. John Peacock was a partner in the firm of Bond, Bromley and Peacock, which claimed to be one of the oldest hatting firms in Denton. He was a captain in the volunteer force raised in Denton during the Napoleonic Wars. The house was taken over by Oldham & Sons Ltd in 1925 and was demolished in 1989.

Peacock Lodge, Denton, before 1900. The house stood at the corner of Annan Street and Lime Grove. It was approached from Hyde Road up a carriage drive lined with lime trees, which have given Lime Grove, built in 1899, its name. The house had extensive grounds, including a lake with swans; Lake Road now covers that area.

Children outside Henry Sidebotham's house, Haughton Green, c. 1890s. This lovely house stood near St Mary's Church by the green. Henry of Haughton Green was the son of William Sidebotham of Hyde. He was a partner with his brother George at Haughton Dale (Meadow) Cotton and Mill, which later became a wire works. He also owned the Nibble & Clink Coal Pit at Haughton Green. Here also lived the local historian Burley Key as a young boy with his family. The house is now demolished.

Huckinbotham House, Glass House Fold, Mill Lane, Haughton. Mill Lane was known as Dark Lane in those days. This house was lived in by a family of one man, two women and one servant in 1851. The house has long since vanished.

Cottages, Lower Haughton. These were in the valley below Haughton Green and were the homes of the workers who quarried the sandstone nearby. This quarry was near the wire works and River Tame at the end of Meadow Lane. The datestone reads 1868.

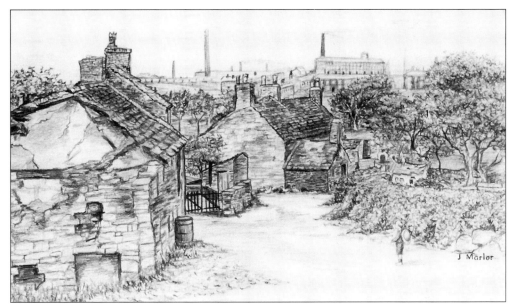

Glass House Fold, Haughton, by Jean Marlor. This group of houses was the home and refuge of a group of seventeenth century Flemish Huguenots, who were fleeing from persecution at home. They were glassmakers by trade and established a flourishing industry by the River Tame in the valley off Dark Lane (now Mill Lane). The site stood across the river from Hyde Hall, Hyde. Their coal-fired furnace and works were excavated in the early 1970s. The family name De Howe is found in various parish registers.

The home of the Scott family in Peel Street, Denton. This fine house stood near the library and was the home of the family who provided Denton with Wilton Street Unitarian Chapel, Russell Scott Day Schools and other community buildings in Wilton Street. Russell and Lawrence Scott were well known figures in Denton and C.P. Scott became the editor of the *Manchester Guardian*. This house was given to the Maternity and Child Welfare Association to use as a welfare centre but it was demolished in 1978 to make way for the M67.

Mawson Hall, King's Road/Corn Hill Lane. This is a front view of the house which stood between the reservoirs and golf courses of Fairfield and Denton. Its gateposts, engraved with its name, are still standing on King's Road. It was at one time home to the Wilson family who were the hat shop owners of Wilson's Hat Factory in Wilton Street. Mawson Hall was demolished in the late 1960s or early 1970s.

Old Thatch, near St Lawrence's Church, Denton, June 1853. These cottages no longer remain but were part of Denton's early history. This is an example of early photography by Joseph Sidebotham. At the right hand end of the cottages was the Millstones, a public house, said to be the oldest alehouse in Denton. It had some disused millstones outside and its entrance was from the graveyard. The cottages were demolished in the 1870s.

The old Parsonage to Denton Chapel, 1853. This early view was taken by Joseph Sidebotham. The parsonage was erected in 1641 by Edward Holland of Denton Hall and here, in the north east corner of the chapel yard, the Reverend John Angier lived until he died in 1677. Later this house became the original Chapel House Inn. It was then divided into cottages and later demolished in 1853, its ground being added to the churchyard.

Broomstair Farm, Hyde Road, Haughton. This painting shows the farm on Broomstair Brow before the new Hyde Road was built, when Old Broom Lane went from Denton, through Haughton and down to the ford over the River Tame. Nearby lay Farmer's Fold (see page 72).

Farmer's Fold, Broomstair, Haughton, 1935. This is a rare view of a group of cottages which stood on the banks of the Tame at the bottom of Broomstair Brow, close to Jet Amber cottages. They were on the old main road, Broom Lane, leading to the ford. There were four cottages forming two sides of a square. In March 1935, a main water pipe burst and flooded them in over a foot of water. Here the occupants are drying out their sodden furniture and fittings.

Acre's Building, Denton. These cottages on the corner of Acre Street and Town Lane are interesting for the notices attached to them. One reads, 'These buildings and upwards of 19,000 square (feet?). Freehold land to be sold or let. Low annual rent. Signed Chas. N. Pinnington, Peel Street, Denton.' Pinnington and Marlor have operated for a long time in Denton as estate agents and are now situated on Manchester Road.

Howard's Lane, Haughton. This lane formed the boundary between Haughton and Denton. On the left can be seen Walker, Ashworth & Linney's offices for their hat works on Ashton Road. All these cottages are long gone and now Howard's Lane runs between the M67 and Oldham & Sons Ltd. Once it was an early route in the area.

Numbers 50-54, Hyde Road, 1938. These cottages are now used as the car park for the Broom House Hotel. They were three small cottages and housed the Dring, Council and Wood families. The Buckley family lived round the corner on Sydall Street and the shop was a grocers called Tomlinson's.

Houses on Stockport Road, Denton, 1969. They are being demolished to make way for Sydall and Sykes Garage. The Jolly Hatter's Public House can be seen on the right. The shop was a grocers run by Topping.

Another view of the demolition, 1969.

## Five

# Church and
# Community

Laying of the foundation stone, St Anne's Church, Haughton, Wednesday 1 September 1880. This is part of Joseph Sidebotham's visual record of the church being built. Edith Watson Sidebotham, his daughter, placed a small hand painted tile of the church beneath the stone. Joseph gave £10,000 to build and fit out the church and then a further £1,700. Fine craftsmen were employed and the church was soon completed and consecrated in 1882. The few houses in the distance give some idea of how the area looked in 1880, before the estate grew.

Denton Chapel and Old Thatch, June 1853, by Joseph Sidebotham. He took various pictures which are the earliest photographs of the chapel which was later renamed St Lawrence's Church. Here it is viewed from the south east with the thatched cottages (see page 70) to the west. The small chancel was added in 1808.

Denton Chapel, June 1853, by Joseph Sidebotham. It shows the vestry door at the south east and the sundial on the wall. Two people sit on the table-top tomb. The old Parsonage (see page 71) is to the right at the east end.

St Anne's Church being erected in May 1882. Another of Joseph's photographs shows details of the building work, step by step. It is a fine, early record of how a church was built. Here is the south side and lych gate. Notice the gentleman with the wagon. Near the doorway can be seen three of the church's six bells.

St Anne's Church and Rectory being constructed in April 1882. This was also taken by Joseph and shows how he meticulously recorded the building of the rectory as well as of the church, the interior of which he also photographed when it was completed.

Another view by Joseph Sidebotham of the erection of St Anne's Church, Haughton, 1880-1882.

Christ Church, Denton, c. 1853. The detailed lithograph shows the fine details of this church which was consecrated in 1853 and was designed by Giles Gilbert Scott. The stone came from the Kerridge Rocks at Macclesfield. It seated 900 and cost £5,100 to build. Until the motorway was built, its day schools stood opposite the church.

Christ Church choir, c. 1893.

St Mary's, Haughton Green. This banner was dedicated on 24 April 1960. It depicts the black and white timber framed church, designed in 1876 by Medland Taylor, the same architect as St Anne's, Haughton. His unusual ideas produced two fine churches for Haughton. The site and much of the cost of St Mary's was provided by the wire works owner James Walton. He had already provided a Sunday school in Meadow Lane in 1858, fulfilling his promise, 'I will build you a school'.

The late Rev. E. V. SCHUSTER.
First Rector S. Mary's Church.

The Reverend E.V. Schuster, first Rector of St Mary's, Haughton Green, from 1876 until 1893.

St Mary's Roman Catholic Church, Market Street, Denton. Here is the original church, called Little Old St Mary's, which was built in 1869 and demolished in 1961 to make way for the new one. The new building is an unusual design, diamond shaped, and nicknamed 'the nun's hat'. Originally it served all Denton and Haughton but there is now another church at Haughton Green, St John Fisher.

First communion at St Mary's, Market Street, Denton.

Here the ladies of Trinity Wesleyan Methodist Chapel, Hyde Road, Denton, wait on a wet day, probably for the Whit Walk procession. They are outside the school which stood on Patterson Street, on the site of the present church.

Two Trees Lane Methodist Chapel, Haughton Green, erected in 1810. Two officials of the church stand in front.

Manchester Road Methodist Church, Denton. This was commonly known as the 'Free Church' as, when it opened, there were no pew rents; they were introduced later. It was opened in 1867 but was demolished to make way for the M67 motorway. The balcony seen at the front of the picture was later moved to the far wall.

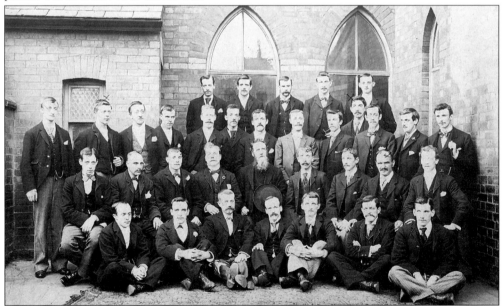

Manchester Road Methodist Church Bible class. From left to right, third row from front: second W. Short (shot shop, Manchester Road), tenth set back, Mr Usher (accountant). Second row from front: third Dan Gee, eighth Joe Stones (sweet shop near station), sixth W. Lambert (Holland Street).

Hope Chapel, Stockport Road, Denton. This is a particularly unusual photograph, as it shows the old Hope Congregational Chapel side by side with its new church hall. Soon the old church would be demolished and a new Hope Church, renamed Hope United Reformed, would be built (see page 11).

Hope Chapel Whit Walk, Stockport Road, Denton, c. 1920s. The ladies of Hope Chapel are passing by their old Sunday school building which was on the corner of Duke Street. It was originally the church until it became the school in 1877. The present church and hall stand on its site (see page 11).

Denton Fire Brigade. This fine fire engine with its crew is taken outside the town yard on the Market Square, where the row of shops and supermarket now stand.

Market Hall, Denton Market Place, c. 1902. The decision to build a market hall was celebrated with a bonfire on the site in October 1893 and a dinner at the King's Head. The tram line gives us the date here, as the traction pole tram from Manchester to Haughton Green ran from 1902.

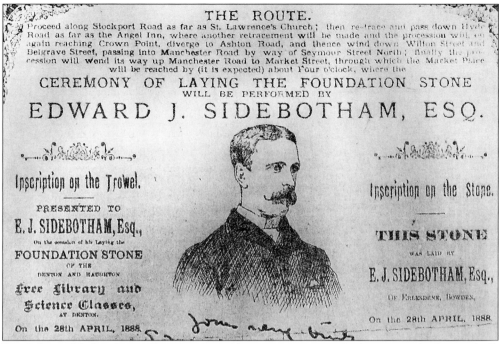

THE ROUTE.

Proceed along Stockport Road as far as St. Lawrence's Church; then re-trace and pass down Hyde Road as far as the Angel Inn, where another retracement will be made and the procession will, on again reaching Crown Point, diverge to Ashton Road, and thence wind down Wilton Street and Belgrave Street, passing into Manchester Road by way of Seymour Street North; finally the procession will wend its way up Manchester Road to Market Street, through which the Market Place will be reached by (it is expected) about Four o'clock, where the

CEREMONY OF LAYING THE FOUNDATION STONE
WILL BE PERFORMED BY

# EDWARD J. SIDEBOTHAM, ESQ.

Inscription on the Trowel.

PRESENTED TO

E. J. SIDEBOTHAM, Esq.,

On the occasion of his Laying the

FOUNDATION STONE

OF THE

DENTON AND HAUGHTON

Free Library and

Science Classes,

AT DENTON.

On the 28th APRIL, 1888.

Inscription on the Stone.

THIS STONE

WAS LAID BY

E. J. SIDEBOTHAM, Esq.,

OF ERLESDENE, BOWDEN,

On the 28th APRIL, 1888.

Free Library, Market Street, Denton, 1888. The two towns never had a purpose-built town hall. The present building was erected as a library and later became the Town Hall when the old Technical School on Peel Street (see page 122) became the Festival Hall and library. Here is the programme for the laying of the foundation stone by Edward J. Sidebotham on 28 April 1888 to open the Free Library in Market Street. A sandwich tea at the People's Hall on Wilton Street ended the celebration.

Entrance to Denton Cemetery, Cemetery Road, Denton, built in 1893. The scene has changed little. Denton opened its cemetery in 1894 when the first interment was of John Yates. The lodge is still there and after near dereliction is now renovated and occupied.

Victoria Park, Denton, *c.* 1900. The park lies behind Market Street. Shown here is the entrance to the bowling green. To the left is the town hall and the building in the middle of the photograph is the presbytery of St Mary's Catholic Church.

Victoria Park, Denton, *c.* 1905. In another view of the park the fine bandstand adorns the centre and the park is full of people in elegant clothes, especially mothers with their perambulators. The Town Hall lies to the top left of the picture and the bowling house is in the centre.

Opening of the Child Welfare Centre, Peel Street, Denton. On the left are Dr William Stewart and Miss A. Walker. Dr Stewart was Medical Officer of Health for Denton for over thirty-five years. He also was head of the St John Ambulance Brigade, teaching first aid with the brigade whilst a doctor in Denton up to the time of his death. The title of Knight of St John was bestowed on him and the new brigade headquarters is named after him.

Dr W. Stewart and ladies of the Maternity and Child Welfare Association, c. 1916. These were the founder members with Dr Stewart, their president. The photograph may have been taken in the grounds of the Russell Scott family home in Peel Street (see page 69). Top row, fourth from right: Mrs Thompson of Thompson's the builders, (see page 17). Front row, second from right: Mrs Wakefield McGill, wife of Dr Wakefield McGill of Huntroyd, Manchester Road, Denton.

Denton Hospital Fund Committee, 1934. Seated first from left: Mr Fred Irwin, JP, who worked at the Town Hall. Third from left: Cllr Fred Worthington, JP, General Secretary of the Hatters' Union. Middle row, fourth from left: Miss Walker of hatters T.W. Walker; fifth from left: Miss Hilda Lennie of the St John Ambulance Brigade. Back row, fourth from left: Cllr Sydney Morrow; fifth from left: Dr Duigenan; sixth from left: Cllr Bardsley, JP.

Parade of St John Ambulance Brigade, c. 1945. They are passing the firm B.H.W. on Stockport Road, Denton, making their way to Stockport Road Playing Fields to be inspected by the late Edwina, Countess of Mountbatten. Every year the procession was held in one of the four divisions of Oldham, Denton, Droylsden or Mossley and this was Denton's turn. Middle row second from front: Miss Vera Lennie (receptionist to Dr Stewart), first in fourth row from front: Mrs Dorothy Thompson.

## *Six*

# Leisure Activities

The Lamb Inn, Haughton Green, *c.* 1890. The landlord, Thomas Moores, is in his shirt sleeves and the array of bowler hats and caps does justice to the two town's hatting industry. The inn began as a beerhouse, maybe in the 1760s. Originally it was part of a row of terraced houses. It closed in 1907 and was demolished in 1926. The site is at the corner of Church Avenue and Haughton Green Road.

The Angel Hotel, Hyde Road, Haughton, *c.* 1950s. Dating from 1597, this coaching inn has been photographed and altered many times (see page 20). Openshaw Brewery owned it at this time. Once the side shown was the back of the inn and the archway to the stables - now filled in - can be seen to the right. In 1979 alterations destroyed much of the early architecture.

The Cricketers' Arms, Haughton Green, *c.* 1908. In the doorway is the landlord at this time, George Greenhalgh. The sign in the lower left window proudly declares, 'Free from Brewery'. Lees Brewery had previously owned the inn which opened in about 1780 and, closed in 1908 to become a house. It was demolished in the 1920s. Its name derives from serving refreshments to locals who had been playing cricket on the green.

The Old Dog Inn, Haughton Green, 7 October 1903. Here too is Haughton Green Post Office on Haughton Green Road. Notice the tram lines. The inn was first a terraced house and then was licensed for selling beer in 1859. John Axon was the landlord at the time of the photograph. The pub underwent alterations in 1964/65 and also in 1982.

The wrestlers of Denton. At first sight this photograph appears to be of a group of swimmers but is, in fact, a group of wrestlers of varying ages. In the 1920s and '30s, Jackie Walsh ran a gym behind The Jolly Hatters on Stockport Road.

Two more Denton wrestlers. On the left is Harry Howarth, known as 'Johnny Simio' and on the right is Andy Goodwin, known as the 'Iron Duke'. Andy also played the accordion in pubs.

Golfers at Denton Golf Club, July, 1930s. Burton drives off the first tee. He and Duncan won both morning and afternoon rounds. To the left of Burton are P. Alliss, G. Cross and G. Duncan. Denton Golf Course opened in 1909.

Ladies' open meeting, Denton Golf Club, June 1935. Nearly 200 players took part in the annual women's open meeting at the club.

Denton Golf Club Fête, 8 July 1916. This is probably the committee which organised it. The club had various fêtes between 1914 and 1918 to raise money for the War Fund; £850 was raised on behalf of the Services War Charities.

Denton Golf Club Fête, 3 July 1915.

Denton Golf Club Fête, 8 July 1916.

Denton Golf Club Fête, on the links, 12 July 1919.

Denton United Hatters Park Football Team, 1934. Hatters Park was behind the Jolly Hatters Public House, Stockport Road. Various teams played in Denton and this was just one of the them. Bevan's Hat Works can be seen in the background.

St Anne's church Football Team, 1913. Many local churches and social clubs had their own sports teams. St Anne's also had a cricket team. From the left, back row: first, Mr Whittaker, second, Charles Clayton. Middle row: first Mr Hibbert, second, Jim Walters (council lamplighter), fifth, Mr Miller. Front row: fifth, Herbert Fletcher.

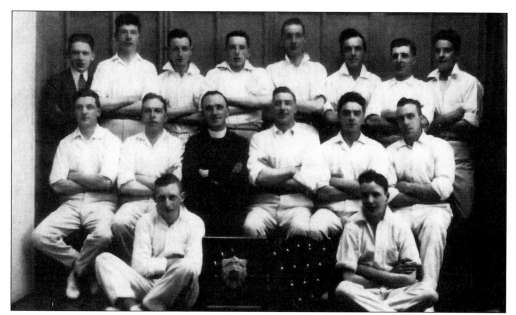

Christ Church Cricket Club, 1920s. They played on a field down Taylor Lane. Back row, left to right: Fred Dickin (scorer), Charles Sainer, Bill Cavanah, -?-, -?-, Bill Dring, Jack Leach, -?-, -?-. Middle row, second from left: Stanley Walker. Front row, left to right: Jack Thomas, John Hulme.

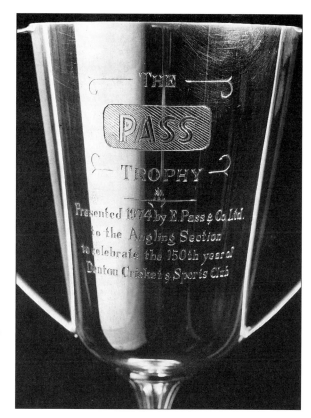

The Pass Trophy for angling, 1974. Pass Engineering Company (see page 55) presented this cup to their anglers to celebrate 150 years of Denton Cricket and Sports Club. Denton Cricket Club is a long established club.

Bowling at the Wilton Arms Hotel, Manchester Road, Denton, early 1900s. There were bowling greens at various public houses in Denton, including The Bowling Green on Manchester Road. These greens are now all gone. Here there is an old tram behind the bowler. It was put there by the landlord so that spectators could view in comfort.

The cinema in Denton. There used to be various cinemas in the town but none now exist. The adverts show the Palace on Ashworth Street and the Barcliff on Ashton Road. The Palace opened in 1912 and could seat nearly 900 people. It closed in 1959 and was demolished in the early 1970s to become the Co-op car park. The Barcliff opened in 1939 as a cinema and closed in 1996 as a bingo hall. There was also the People's Hall on Prestwich Street. It was a cinema from 1908 to 1958 and is now a roller skating rink. It boasted the slogan, 'Where sound is sound'.

Denton Original Prize Band in Victoria Park bandstand, Denton, *c.* 1900. In 1899 they won the Nelson Challenge Cup. They were winners of the Crystal Palace 1,000 Guinea Challenge Cup in London and of £75 in a competition open to Great Britain and the Colonies on 21 July 1900.

Denton Brotherhood *Minstrels*. Founded in 1906 on the initiative of the Revd W.W. Hollings, the Wesleyan minister, the Brotherhood met in the Co-operative Hall and later a cottage was converted into a social institute. There was a savings bank, book, cycling, football and rambling clubs and a choir led by Arnold Eaton.

St Lawrence's Musical Society, early 1920s. This photograph shows just one of many of the amateur theatrical and musical companies flourishing in Denton and Haughton. Here the ladies of the Mothers' Union performed *Ye Olde Village Wedding*, a Yorkshire dialect sketch.

The First Haughton Green (St Mary's) Scouts. This photograph represents just one of the many groups of Scouts, Cubs, Guides, Brownies and Church Lads' Brigades which were run by the local churches.

# Seven
# At Peace and at War

Hope Congregational Church Band of Hope, c. 1908. They are on the market ground. The cottages forming Nos. 21-27 Stockport Road, Denton, can be seen in the background and were demolished in the early 1930s. The Gardeners' Arms is top left. The band was formed by Sam Royds and Tom Thornhill.

Works trip to Blackpool from Denton Station, 23 June 1962.

Ladies in a Whit Walk procession, c. 1900. These women were dressed up for this special occasion. Behind them is Denton Town Hall and to the right is the wall of the Town Yard. The Town Hall is decked out with bunting. The United Service of churches was always held in the market square, which is to the right of these ladies who are probably from St Anne's Church.

Whit Friday on the Market Ground, 1960s. The Town Hall can be seen in the background and the post office and public conveniences are to the left. The Town Yard is to the right of the Town Hall and the early market huts can be seen on the market ground. The crowds are there for the United Churches' Service. Notice the banners of the different churches.

Outside Carmel Church, Seymour Street, Denton. These people are assembling to join the Whit Walks. This church was started in the late 1940s over a shop on Manchester Road by Pastor Alfred Webb of Hyde. He was followed by Pastor Adcock, owner of Multiple Winding. They moved to the Seymour Street site in the early 1950s and have improved the building since then.

Tram strike, Sunday 20 October 1900. This unusual photograph shows the workers with their shunting poles and a banner proclaiming 'Society of Railway Servants of England, Ireland, Scotland. Warrington Branch'. On the right, on the corner of Annan Street, is the old Silver Springs Arms shortly before demolition. Beyond the public house is the Co-op building. The strikers were marching from the tram depot on Ashton Road.

Walks to commemorate the Silver Jubilee of King George and Queen Mary, 6 May 1935. Here are members of Trinity Methodist Church on Hyde Road, Denton. The row of houses in the background is now the site of the Job Centre.

Rose Queen, Christ Church, Denton, 1956. Many of the local churches maintained the tradition of having an annual Rose Queen and her retinue. Here is Margaret Jarratt as the Rose Queen with Dorothy Baxter (far right) as one of her attendants. The lady on the left is Mrs Gallimore.

Rose Queen, Christ Church, Denton, 1954. As well as raising money for charities, the Rose Queen and her retinue paraded in local carnivals and processions such as the Whit Friday Walks, as seen here. The procession is just passing Joseph Howe & Sons Hat Works and their houses on Annan Street. (see pages 24 and 26)

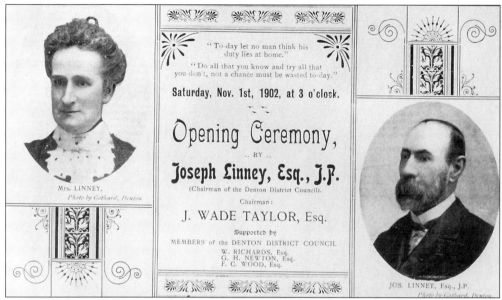

Bazaar at Christ Church, Denton, 1 November 1902. This is part of the programme booklet for the bazaar which was very popular and an excellent method of fund raising in the early 1900s. A well known local personality always opened the bazaar. On this occasion it was Joseph Linney and his wife. He was a partner in the hat works, Walker, Ashworth & Linney (see pages 27 and 28).

Bazaar at St Anne's Church, Haughton, 1910. Here we can see the trouble people took to dress up for the occasion. They are lined up in front of St Anne's Day Schools. In the centre is the rector, Revd William Parrett. Behind the group on the right can be seen the beautiful mosaic of St Anne with her daughter, Mary. Above it is the coat of arms of the Sidebotham family who provided the church and school.

Coronation street party, 2 June 1953, Denton. This was held to celebrate the coronation of Queen Elizabeth II; it represents just one of the countless such parties held in the streets of Denton and all over England. Television was just becoming affordable and many families in a road squeezed into one of their neighbours' houses to watch the coronation on the tiny screen of their new TV.

The Coronation, June 1953. Here is the display proudly decorating the balcony of the Liberal Club, Manchester Road, Denton. There are also Conservative and Labour Clubs in the town.

Cutting the first sod of earth for Denton Swimming Baths, 24 January 1973. Mr Fred Worthington is digging the turf, watched by the Chairman of Denton District Council, Mr J. Devaney. Cllr Worthington was also General Secretary of the Felt Hatters and Trimmers Unions. It was his dream for fifty years that Denton should have a swimming baths. These were officially opened by the Olympic swimmer Anita Lonsbrough, MBE on 3 July 1975.

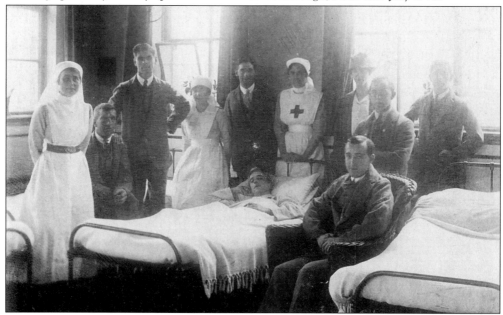

Denton Council School, Duke Street, was converted to a military hospital during the First World War. Shown here are some of the wards with nurses and wounded soldiers. During the Second World War it was used as a first aid station, run by the St John Ambulance Brigade.

110

Albert Hill, VC. Private Hill of No. 45 High Street, Denton, was the only hat worker to win the Victoria Cross in the First World War. Here he is seen seated in his uniform among his fellow workers at Wilson's Hat Works, Wilton Street, Denton; he had already been welcomed at the Town Hall and mobbed by delighted crowds. The following day he visited Wilson's, where he had worked as a planker. He had also won the French Croix de Guerre and the Russian Cross of St George of the First Class.

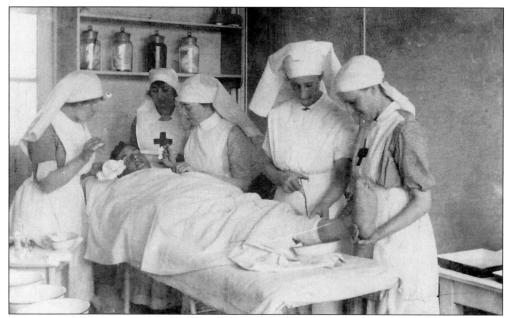

Operating theatre in the Military Hospital, Duke Street School, Denton, 1914-18. Second from the left is Hannah Broadbent with the Red Cross emblem on her apron. The nurse next to the end on the right is Edith Eaton.

'At the nineteenth hole!', Denton Golf Course, 18 October 1940. A German bomber plane jettisoned its last bomb on the clubhouse. Luckily the club had closed half an hour beforehand and Mr Tooke, the club steward, and his wife escaped from the rubble. The next day he returned to rescue his black tom cat called Mutt. Mr Tooke had to crawl in and retrieve the dust-covered cat. A second jettisoned bomb made a crater thirty feet away across the fairway of the tenth hole.

Arnold Thorley, Second World War. Mr Thorley was the last owner of the firm, Turner Atherton & Co. Ltd. The firm invented and produced hat machinery. (see page 50)

Ambulance donated by Mr and Mrs Clayton, c. 1939. The presentation of this ambulance afforded this impressive line-up. ARP Wardens, St John Ambulance workers and nurses joined the mayor and other officials. The mayor and his mayoress were Cllr W. West and his wife. On Mrs West's left is Dr William Stewart, Medical Officer for Health in Denton, who did so much for the town. (see pages 89-90)

German bomb, Hyde Hall Farm, 17 July 1942. This bomb had lain twenty-five feet down in a field, unexploded, since the Christmas blitz of 1940. It was displayed on the bandstand in Victoria Park, Denton, for a month to raise money for the National Air-Raid Distress Fund. Naturally it had been defused but its fins had been restored by the Progressive Engineering Co. Ltd.

ARP Demolition Squad, 1940. This group worked for Denton Urban District Council and is seen here working at Beight Bank, off Stockport Road. These houses were near where the sewage works are now located. The man nearest the camera is W. Jarvis.

## Eight
# At School and at Home

St Anne's Schools, Haughton, 1888. The Sidebotham family gave the land for a school to complete their gift of a church and rectory (see pages 75, 78, 79). Here is an architect's drawing showing the front of the schools with their fine mosaic to St Anne, the Sidebotham coat of arms and stained glass windows. The schools were originally a church National school, having a senior section from 1906 and becoming a state school in 1953. A disastrous fire in 1936 caused major damage.

St Anne's School, Haughton, 1939. Here is an infants class with their headmistress, Miss Livia Snelson, who was head of the infants' school from 1906 until 1945. The partition wall could be folded back to make the school hall larger.

'The Iron School', Haughton Dale, 1858. This iron building was known by its appropriate nickname instead of its proper name of Haughton Dale School. It was built in 1858 by the wire works owner, James Walton, as a recreational and educational centre for his work people and for a day and Sunday school. Notice the unusual air vents at the top of the building. The school was on Meadow Lane and was demolished in 1905.

Class Standard 4, St Lawrence's Day Schools, May 1927. This school was on Stockport Road and had both infants and juniors. The land was loaned in 1853 by the mineowner Jacob Fletcher Fletcher to build a replacement school. The original had been built in 1769 near St Lawrence's Church. Greswell School on Percy Road later replaced the Stockport Road building.

St Lawrence's Day Schools. A group of infant children dressed up for a special event, possibly the Whit Walks. They are pictured outside the school. Second from left is Alice McMinn, née Godley.

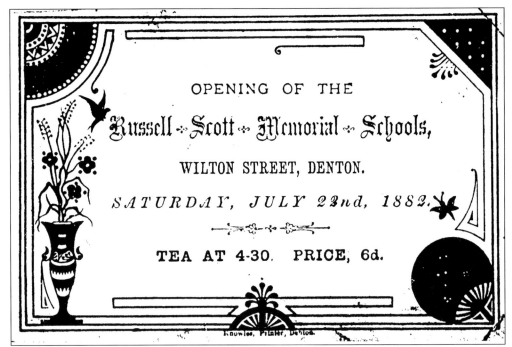

The invitation card for the opening of the Russell Scott Memorial Schools, Wilton Street, Denton, 22 July 1882. Many of the schools were endowed by local families who owned the mines, mills or hat works. These schools were built by the Scott family to complete their gift of the Unitarian Chapel and Sunday school. Russell and Lawrence Scott were well known locally, Lawrence being the minister of the chapel.

Russell Scott Memorial Schools, Wilton Street, Denton, 1930s. The headmaster was Mr Pitt. The schools were opened in 1882 by Mr R. Peacock MP of Gorton Hall. Mrs Russell Scott defrayed the cost in memory of her husband. Her sons were the chapel's minister, Lawrence, and the editor of the *Manchester Guardian*, C.P. Scott. The schools were demolished when the M67 was built and a new school was provided on a different site.

Christ Church Day Schools, Denton, *c.* 1848. Here is a lithograph of the schools on Manchester Road, opposite the church. They were built in 1848 by the Revd Richard Greswell whose father was the Perpetual Curate of St Lawrence's Church. They cost £1,750 and preceded the church itself by five years.

Christ Church Day Schools, Denton, 1979. This is the sad sight of the schools derelict and being demolished to make way for the M67 Motorway.

Christ Church Day Schools, Denton, 1903. The headmaster was Mr Tattersall, seen here on the left with the class teacher on the right. Notice the bows and fancy collars of the girls' dresses and the collars of the boys.

Class V, 1938, Christ Church Day Schools, Denton. On the right is Mr Briggs, the headmaster. On the left is the class teacher, Mrs Partridge.

Haughton Dale Mill School Certificate, 1889. This certificate is a sample of the many colour-fully illustrated awards for progress at school.

Methodist Free Church Schools, Denton, coronation year, 1902. The headmaster was Mr Greenhalgh. This school opened in 1867 for Manchester Road Methodist Church, which followed in 1868. It closed in 1913 but was used temporarily between 1945 and 1953.

Denton Technical School, Peel Street, Denton, *c.* 1930-38. The present Festival Hall is housed in what used to be the Technical School which opened in 1896. Here is the gymnasium which, in the early 1950s, cost £500 to convert into the Festival Hall.

The gymnasium, Denton Technical School, Peel Street, Denton.

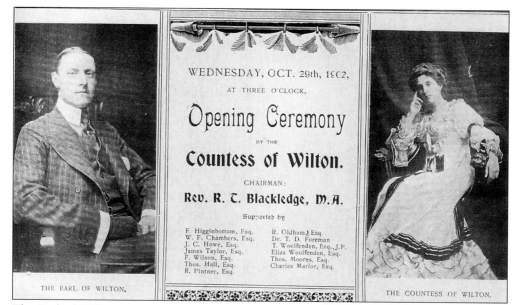

WEDNESDAY, OCT. 29th, 1902,

AT THREE O'CLOCK,

# Opening Ceremony

BY THE

# Countess of Wilton.

CHAIRMAN:

## Rev. R. C. Blackledge, M.A.

Supported by

F. Higginbottom, Esq.  
W. F. Chambers, Esq.  
J. C. Howe, Esq.  
James Taylor, Esq.  
F. Wilson, Esq.  
Thos. Hall, Esq.  
R. Pintner, Esq.  

R. Oldham, Esq.  
Dr. T. D. Foreman  
T. Woolfenden, Esq., J.P.  
Elias Woolfenden, Esq.  
Thos. Moores, Esq.  
Charles Marlor, Esq.  

THE EARL OF WILTON.

THE COUNTESS OF WILTON.

The Earl of Wilton and his Countess, 1902. The De Denton family built and lived at the original Denton Hall in Windmill Lane, Denton. They married into the Holland family who also lived at Denton Hall. The Hollands then married into the Egertons, who later became the Earls of Wilton and who came to own much land in Denton. Here the Earl and his wife are to open the bazaar at Christ Church, Denton.

Joseph Watson Sidebotham on the occasion of his marriage to his wife Marion. His father was the Edward Joseph Sidebotham, who owned mines and mills in Haughton, built St Anne's Church and Rectory and took many rare photographs of Denton and Haughton in the early 1850s. Joseph Watson was himself organist at St Anne's and gave the land for the schools. He was MP for Hyde.

123

The founders of Walker, Ashworth & Linney Ltd, 29 January 1926. They are seated at The Limes, Manchester Road, Denton, later to become the home of the curate of Christ Church. They founded their hat works in 1867 (see pages 27-8) and traded together for over fifty years. From left to right: Thomas Walker, James Ashworth, Samuel Ashworth, Joseph Linney.

The Reverend Lawrence Scott, Minister of Wilton Street Unitarian Chapel. His family generously gave Denton many buildings, including this church, schools, the People's Hall and the Lads' Club. He was the church's first minister and went on to celebrate his Jubilee as its minister. He died in 1930 aged 83. (see page 118)

James Walton, 1803-1883, was another employer and benefactor of Haughton. He gave the town its 'Iron School' (see page 116) and St Mary's Anglican Church (see page 81), and owned the wire works in Meadow Lane, which had previously been a cotton mill. He retired to Wales where he had an estate and became both High Sheriff of Montgomeryshire in 1877 and a JP. He died in 1883.

Mr and Mrs Joseph Woolfenden with their family. In 1830 Joseph Woolfenden founded his hat works at his farm at Dane Bank. His four sons assisted him and soon they built a large factory, with housing for workers, managers and themselves, plus a shop and public house. Today only the owners' houses still stand at High Bank, as well as the original farmhouse.

Group at top of Wilton Street, Denton, early 1900s. This photograph shows a collection of children and their families. It is remarkable for the array of fashion it displays.

Trip to Southport, July 1925. The charabanc is taking a group of Co-op workers from Denton.

Trip from Charles Marlor's Hat Works, Taylor Lane, Denton. The smartly dressed men all sport bowler hats, as befits members of a hatting firm. They are departing from John Street, Haughton, by horse and cart.

Journey's end. A fitting end for them - and for us - is the arrival at their destination at New Pool.

# Acknowledgements

We should like to thank the following organisations and individuals for giving permission for their photographs to be included in this book. We have tried to locate everyone and apologise if anyone has been omitted.

Denton Local History Society Archive

Members of the society including Allan Arrowsmith, Jill and Paul Cronin, Jean and Joe Marlor, Marion and Geoffrey Pilcher, Frank Rhodes and Colin Yearsley.

Officials of Christ Church, St Anne's Church (the Sidebotham Collection), St Mary's RC Church and Wilton Street Chapel.

Staff at Stalybridge Local Studies Library.

The Burley Key Collection.

Ronald Bromley, Alfred Brown, Kenneth Burton (Stuart Ibbotson Collection), Arthur Edwards, Dennis Gill, Mr Gott, Jean Halliday, Mrs Mitchell, Gordon Ollerenshaw, George Taylor, Dorothy Thompson, Frederick Whiteside and all who have donated or loaned photographs to the society over the years.